RAINBOW BOWLS

Easy, delicious ways to #EatTheRainbow

RAINBOW BOWLS

Easy, delicious ways to #EatTheRainbow

NIKI WEBSTER

@rebelrecipes

POP PRESS

Contents

Introduction

Hi, and thank you for picking up this copy of Rainbow Bowls!

I'm Niki and I'm a plant-based cook, cookbook author and veg obsessive. Since starting my blog Rebel Recipes in 2016 it's been my aim to share vibrant meals centred around vegetables. And to gently challenge people's perceptions that plant-based meals are boring or lacking in flavour or texture. I hope I've gone a little way in doing this but there's still more to do...

In Rainbow Bowls I'm bringing you 40 vibrantly healthy and delicious meals in a bowl, all showcasing how amazing vegetables and fruit can be and packed full of enticing flavours, textures and colours. If you need inspiration for easy and accessible ways to eat more veg, you've come to the right place.

You may have heard the term 'Eating the rainbow' but what are the benefits? Eating a broad spectrum of colourful fruit and vegetables

throughout the day means you get a variety of vitamins and nutrients, which helps maintain a healthy diet. That's why I love them AND they taste fantastic.

In this book, you're going to find lots of sustaining bowls of comfort food like curries, soups and stews – meals which make you feel good. While you might not find a rainbow in every meal, these dishes will help you to eat a range of coloured fruit and vegetables throughout your day to get that all-important broad range of vitamins and minerals into your diet. You'll also find lots of tasty spices as that's what really makes vegetable-based dishes come alive with flavour.

I love to use veg or pulses as a base instead of the more traditional rice/pasta, etc. Not only does this add tons of flavour, it's also way more nutritious as it's adding more plant-based protein and/or vitamins and minerals and fibre.

I really hope you enjoy cooking from this book.

Much love, Niki xxx

Breakfast Bowls

SWEET

Creamy Tahini Date Porridge with Roast Fruit

•

Baked Grain Bowl with Blackberries and Maple

•

Matcha, Coconut and Cacao Overnight Oats

•

Banana and Pecan Granola Bowl with
Caramelised Bananas

SAVOURY

Lazy Weekend Brunch Bowl with Mushrooms,
Greens, Harissa Hummus and Juicy Tomatoes

•

Pea and Buckwheat Crêpe Bowl with
Creamy Greens and Tofu

•

Spicy Tomato Hash

•

Chickpea and Mushroom Rice

Creamy Tahini Date Porridge with Roast Fruit

Serves 1
Prep time 5 minutes
Cooking time 20–25 minutes

For the roast fruit
2 nectarines or peaches, stoned and sliced
1 tbsp maple syrup
½ tsp orange extract

For the porridge
45g jumbo oats
250ml plant-based milk, plus extra to loosen if needed
2 Medjool dates, pitted and finely chopped
1 tbsp tahini
1 tsp vanilla extract

Toppings
Plant-based Greek-style yoghurt
1–2 tbsp chopped nuts – almonds or hazelnuts

Porridge is one of the best ways to start the day – healthy, delicious and never boring because of the countless flavour combinations. This version is a little different with the addition of creamy nutty tahini and sweetened by jammy dates. The gooey, warm roast fruit with the creamy oats is just lovely. You can use any seasonal stone fruit here – plums, nectarines, peaches and apricots are all delicious.

Preheat the oven to 180°C.

To make the roast fruit, add the nectarines to a small baking tray and drizzle with the maple syrup and orange extract.

Bake for 20–25 minutes until soft and caramelising.

To make the porridge, add the oats, milk, dates, tahini and vanilla to a small saucepan and simmer on a low heat, stirring continuously for a few minutes, until the porridge has absorbed the milk but is not too dry.

Remove from the heat and serve the porridge topped with the roast fruit, yoghurt, chopped nuts and more plant-based milk to loosen.

Breakfast Bowls

Baked Grain Bowl with Blackberries and Maple

Serves 2
Prep time 5 minutes
Cooking time 12 minutes

80g rolled oats
1 tbsp ground flaxseed
2 tbsp rye or wheat flakes
5 tbsp ground almonds
1 tbsp chopped nuts and/
  or seeds, such as
  almonds, hazelnuts,
  sunflower or pumpkin
  seeds
½ tsp ground cinnamon or
  mixed spice (optional)
1 tsp baking powder
1–2 tbsp coconut or light
  soft brown sugar
250ml almond milk
1 tsp vanilla extract
2 tbsp plant-based Greek-
  style yoghurt, plus extra
  to serve
Black sesame seeds to
  serve (optional)

For the warm berries
150g blackberries
1 tbsp maple syrup
Splash of water

Baked oats are pure comfort. I've added in a few healthy but delicious ingredients here: ground flaxseed and some rye or wheat flakes for extra fibre. All you need to do is mix, then bake for 12 minutes. Easy. The warm blackberries and creamy cold yoghurt are the perfect accompaniment.

Preheat the oven to 180°C.

Add all the dry ingredients to a large bowl and mix to combine, then add the almond milk, vanilla extract and yoghurt. Mix everything well. Divide the mixture between two ovenproof dishes, then bake for about 12 minutes until golden brown.

Meanwhile, to make the warm berries, add the berries, maple syrup and water to a saucepan and heat gently until the berries have broken down a little.

Serve the baked grains topped with the warm berries, a scoop of creamy yoghurt and a few black sesame seeds if you fancy.

Tip
If you don't have any grain flakes, you can add whole oats instead.

Matcha, Coconut and Cacao Overnight Oats

Serves 1
Prep time 5 minutes, plus overnight soaking

5 tbsp oats of your choice
½ tsp vanilla extract
    or powder
200ml plant-based milk,
    plus extra if needed
½ tsp matcha powder
2 tbsp coconut yoghurt
1 tbsp cacao nibs or dairy-
    free chocolate chips
1–2 tsp maple syrup

Topping options
1 tbsp chopped pistachios
Berries
Seeds

It may seem unusual to add tea to your oats, but the flavour of matcha works beautifully with the creamy vanilla oats and the little bursts of cacao nibs. The matcha also turns the oats a lovely shade of pale green as well as providing antioxidants, vitamins and a subtle energy boost. You do need a little sweetness with this one, so I recommend adding a little maple syrup.

To make the overnight oats, add the oats, vanilla and milk to a Mason jar or bowl and mix to combine. Cover and leave to soak overnight in the fridge.

Remove the oats from the fridge and stir in the matcha, yoghurt, cacao nibs and maple syrup.

Spoon into a bowl and add more plant-based milk to loosen if needed. Add toppings of your choice and enjoy.

Banana and Pecan Granola Bowl with Caramelised Bananas

Serves 2
Prep time 10 minutes
Cooking time 45 minutes

2 tbsp coconut oil
4 tbsp maple syrup
2 very ripe
   medium bananas
1 tsp almond extract
100g oats of your choice
3 tbsp unsweetened
   desiccated coconut
2 tbsp ground almonds
3 tbsp sunflower seeds
3 tbsp chopped nuts, such
   as hazelnuts or almonds
40g pecans
Pinch of sea salt

For the caramelised bananas
2 unpeeled bananas
1 tbsp coconut oil

To serve
Coconut yoghurt
1 tsp maple syrup (optional)
Pinch of thyme (optional)

This tasty breakfast recipe is all about bananas. They are baked into the granola, which is then served with the amazing caramelised bananas. If you haven't tried them, you're in for a treat as they become sticky, warm and even sweeter. The granola makes about 4–6 portions, so store it in an airtight container for a speedy breakfast or snack.

Preheat the oven to 180°C.

Blend the coconut oil, maple syrup, bananas and almond extract in a blender until smooth.

Add all the dry ingredients to a large bowl and mix well. Add the wet mixture to the bowl and stir well to combine.

Line a large baking tray with baking paper and then tip the granola mix on to the tray and flatten out. Bake for 25 minutes until starting to brown. Carefully flip over on the tray, then return to the oven and bake for a further 15 minutes (until you get a nice brown colour).

Leave to cool before breaking into smaller chunks, then store in an airtight container for up to 1 week (if not eating straight away).

To make the caramelised bananas, chop off the top end of each of the bananas, then carefully slice through the middle lengthways. Now, peel the bananas.

Melt the coconut oil in a pan on a medium heat. Add the banana slices and fry in the oil on one side for 1-2 minutes until browned, then flip over to caramelise the other side for another 1-2 minutes.

Serve the granola with yoghurt, caramelised bananas, a drizzle of maple syrup and a pinch of thyme if you fancy.

Lazy Weekend Brunch Bowl with Mushrooms, Greens, Harissa Hummus and Juicy Tomatoes

Serves 2
Prep time 15 minutes
Cooking time 25 minutes

300g cherry
   tomatoes
4 portobello
   mushrooms, whole
2 tbsp olive oil
100g asparagus, with
   ends removed
100g spring greens
Squeeze of lemon juice
1 avocado, flesh sliced
2 tsp toasted
   sunflower seeds
Sea salt and black pepper

For the harissa hummus
400g can chickpeas,
   drained and rinsed
1 garlic clove, peeled
2 tbsp tahini
1 tbsp harissa paste
2 tbsp plant-based
   natural yoghurt
Juice of ½ lemon
1 tbsp extra virgin olive oil

This is one for the weekend when you've got a little more time to cook, sit down and enjoy a lazy brunch. It's easy to grab toast or cereal in the morning, which is all good, but when I have a little more time I love to cook up a little feast like this – delicious and packed with veggies which you can feel pretty smug about. I love this served with big slabs of fresh bread.

Preheat the oven to 180°C.

Place the cherry tomatoes and mushrooms on a baking tray, drizzle with 1 tablespoon of olive oil and scatter over some salt. Roast for 20–25 minutes or until the tomatoes are soft and oozing.

Meanwhile, make the harissa hummus. Add all the ingredients to a food processor and blitz until very smooth and creamy – this should take about 2 minutes.

Add the asparagus and the remaining 1 tablespoon of oil to a pan or griddle pan and char for 4–5 minutes, then add the greens and allow to wilt for 1–2 minutes. Squeeze in the lemon juice and season well.

To serve, use the harissa hummus as a base for the roast tomatoes and mushrooms, asparagus and greens, sliced avocado and toasted seeds.

Pea and Buckwheat Crêpe Bowl with Creamy Greens and Tofu

Serves 2
Prep time 10 minutes plus 10 minutes resting
Cooking time 20 minutes

For the crêpes
100g buckwheat
  or rye flour
175ml water
1 tsp apple cider vinegar
140g frozen peas,
  defrosted by running
  under a hot tap in a sieve
½ tsp garlic granules
2 tbsp extra virgin olive oil
Sea salt and black pepper

For the filling
1 tbsp olive oil
4 spring onions, sliced
2 broccoli spears or greens
  of your choice, such as
  sugar snap peas, kale
  and/or asparagus
½ tsp garlic granules
120g firm smoked tofu
  or natural firm tofu,
  drained well and cut
  into 1cm cubes
100g baby spinach,
  shredded
2 tbsp plant-based natural
  or Greek-style yoghurt,
  plus extra to serve
4 tbsp nutritional yeast
Juice of ½ lemon

A savoury breakfast or brunch packed with healthy plant-based protein. Sweet green peas are blended into the crêpe batter, which is then filled with creamy smoky tofu and greens – healthy and incredibly tasty. A vibrant green bowl of goodness.

To make the crêpe batter, add the flour, water, vinegar, peas, garlic granules and 1 tablespoon of oil to your food processor with ½ teaspoon of salt and a twist of black pepper and blitz to a thick batter. Set aside for 10 minutes.

Add the remaining 1 tablespoon of oil to the base of a small, non-stick frying pan on a medium heat. Add 2 heaped tablespoons of the batter to the pan and swirl around the bottom with a spoon so you get an even crêpe. Cook for about 2 minutes until there are bubbles in the crepe and you can lift it over to flip easily. Flip and cook on the other side for 30 seconds–1 minute. Remove from the pan and place on a plate, then cover with a clean cloth to keep warm. Repeat the process with the remaining batter – you should have 4 pancakes in total.

Meanwhile, to make the filling, add the oil to a medium saucepan on a medium heat and fry the spring onions for 5–6 minutes until soft. Add the broccoli and garlic granules and fry for a further 2–3 minutes. Then add the tofu and spinach and cook for 5-6 minutes. Add the yoghurt, nutritional yeast and lemon juice and season well.

Serve the crêpes with the creamy greens and a drizzle of yoghurt on top.

Spicy Tomato Hash

Serves 2
Prep time 10 minutes
Cooking time 45 minutes

400g potatoes, scrubbed
2 tbsp olive oil
2 tbsp extra virgin olive oil
1 large red onion,
    roughly chopped
3 garlic cloves, sliced
1 tsp cumin seeds
1 tsp ground coriander
2 tsp smoked paprika
250g cherry
    tomatoes, chopped
50g slow-roasted
    tomatoes, chopped,
    or 3 tbsp sun-dried
    tomato paste
Pinch of chilli flakes
1 avocado, flesh chopped
    into chunks
Sea salt and black pepper
Fresh thyme leaves

This is inspired by shakshuka, with the addition of crispy potatoes and minus the eggs. The tomatoes are sticky and jammy and just perfect with the crispy fried potatoes. I've topped them with creamy avocado and would eat this for breakfast every day if I could.

Add the potatoes to a large pan of salted boiling water. Boil the potatoes until just tender, then drain and allow to cool.

Chop the potatoes into 2cm cubes and add to a frying pan along with the olive oil and a pinch of salt. Fry on a medium heat for about 10 minutes until super crispy and browning on all sides.

Meanwhile, to make the spicy tomatoes, add the extra virgin olive oil to a large frying pan on a medium heat. Add the onion and fry for 8–10 minutes until soft and browning. Add the garlic and fry for a further minute. Now, add the spices and cook for a minute or so. Then add the cherry and slow-roasted tomatoes and cook for a further 5 minutes until they are softened. Season really well and add the chilli flakes.

Serve the tomatoes topped with the crispy potatoes, avocado and some fresh thyme leaves.

Chickpea and Mushroom Rice

Serves 2
Prep time 10 minutes
Cooking time 40 minutes

1 tbsp olive oil
1 onion, sliced
1 tsp medium curry powder
½ tsp ground turmeric
½ tsp smoked paprika
2 garlic cloves, sliced
150g basmati rice, rinsed
750ml hot vegetable stock
100g chestnut
    mushrooms, sliced
2 large handfuls of spring
    greens, chopped
400g can chickpeas,
    drained and rinsed
2 tbsp fresh chives,
    chopped
2 tbsp fresh dill, chopped,
    plus extra for topping
Juice of ½ lemon
Sea salt and black pepper

**For the dill and
mint yoghurt**
4 tbsp plant-based
    natural yoghurt
Handful of fresh mint
    and dill, shredded
Large pinch of sea salt
Pinch of chilli flakes

This is a very comforting and nourishing khichari-inspired rice and pulse breakfast dish which provides complete plant-based protein from the rice and chickpeas. It's a brilliant and very sustaining breakfast or brunch, but it's also a great lunch option too, ideally served with some veggie curry. The dill and mint dip adds lovely fresh flavours and a creamy texture, so I urge you to dollop generously on top.

Heat the oil in a saucepan, add the onion and cook on a medium heat for 8–10 minutes until soft. Add the garlic, spices and rice to the pan and stir to combine. Add half the stock and simmer for 15–20 minutes until the rice is soft, adding more stock as necessary (like a risotto).

Meanwhile, to make the dill and mint yoghurt, add all the ingredients to a small bowl and mix to combine.

Finally, add the mushrooms and greens to the rice and cook for 10 minutes. When the mushrooms and greens are cooked and all the stock has been absorbed, add the chickpeas, chives and dill. Stir to combine. Season well and serve with small dollops of the dill and mint yoghurt, a squeeze of lemon and some fresh dill.

Salads + Soups

Crushed Potato, Fennel and Shallot
Salad with Red Walnut Pesto

•

Spiced Roast Squash, Caramelised
Onion and Rocket Salad

•

Charred Green Veg and Toasted
Sourdough Salad

•

Griddled Aubergine and Peanut Salad

•

Roast Tomato and Pepper Soup with Zhoug

•

Spiced Lentil and Tomato Soup

•

Hearty Sweet Potato Soup

Crushed Potato, Fennel and Shallot Salad with Red Walnut Pesto

Serves 2
Prep time 10 minutes
Cooking time 1 hour 5 minutes

For the roast veg
500g new or baby potatoes
1 fennel bulb, sliced
2 echalion shallots, halved or quartered
3 tbsp olive oil
Sea salt and black pepper

For the red pesto
100g walnut halves
250g sun-blush or sun-dried tomatoes in oil, drained
30g fresh basil
1 garlic clove, peeled
4 tbsp nutritional yeast
3 tbsp extra virgin olive oil
Juice of ½ lemon
50ml water

Toppings
Fresh dill and mint leaves
Cherry tomatoes, halved
Drizzle of extra virgin olive oil

This is a pretty special warm salad. Crushed potatoes with their roasted crispness are always fantastic and when combined with sticky caramelised shallots and fennel they are simply delicious! The red pesto is very addictive, use it on everything – sandwiches, toast, pasta, roast veg – it's incredible.

Preheat the oven to 180°C.

To make the roast veg, first, boil the potatoes in a pan of salted boiling water for 15 minutes. You want them to be cooked through but still hold their shape when lightly crushed. Drain the potatoes, allow to cool a little, then place them in a large baking tray and lightly crush using a fork.

Add the fennel and shallots to the baking tray, drizzle over the olive oil and season with 1 teaspoon of salt and a good twist of black pepper and toss to cover the vegetables. Bake for about 50 minutes, turning the potatoes halfway through cooking.

Meanwhile, to make the red pesto, dry toast the walnuts in a pan for 2–3 minutes until lightly toasted, being careful not to let them burn.

Add all the pesto ingredients to a food processor with ½ teaspoon of salt and a twist of black pepper and blitz to a chunky paste.

Serve the roast veg on a bed of the red pesto. Top with fresh herbs, cherry tomatoes and a drizzle of extra virgin olive oil.

Spiced Roast Squash, Caramelised Onion and Rocket Salad

Serves 2
Prep time 10 minutes
Cooking time 1 hour

1 tsp ground coriander
1 tsp sweet paprika
½ tsp ground allspice
2 tbsp olive oil
1 small butternut squash,
  cut into 6 lengthways
  and deseeded
2 tbsp hazelnuts
Big handful of rocket
2 tbsp sun-blush tomatoes
Sea salt

For the caramelised onions
2 tbsp olive oil
½ tsp cumin seeds
2 red onions, sliced into
  half moons

For the dressing
1 tsp za'atar
1 tbsp extra virgin olive oil
Juice of ½ lemon
1 tsp maple syrup

Butternut squash roasted in warming spices until crispy on the outside and tender inside, served with sticky caramelised onions and a rocket, sun-blush tomato and toasted hazelnut salad. This dish is perfect for any time of the year and is substantial enough for a main meal. I love to serve it with some fresh warm bread and good-quality extra virgin olive oil.

Preheat the oven to 180°C.

Mix the spices and olive oil in a jar to combine. Place the butternut squash on a baking tray, pour over the spicy oil and toss to mix. Bake for 45 minutes–1 hour until the squash is tender inside and caramelised on the outside.

Meanwhile, make the caramelised onions. Add the oil, cumin seeds, onions and a pinch of salt to a small pan and fry very slowly on a low heat for 30–40 minutes until soft and caramelised.

To make the dressing, add all the ingredients to a jar with a pinch of salt, replace the lid and shake to combine.

To serve, dry toast the hazelnuts in a frying pan on a medium heat for 2–3 minutes until lightly toasted.

Serve the roast squash with the caramelised onions, rocket, toasted hazelnuts, sun-blush tomatoes and dressing.

Charred Green Veg and Toasted Sourdough Salad

Serves 2
Prep time 10 minutes
Cooking time 15 minutes

1 tbsp olive oil
75g asparagus, woody
    ends removed
80g sugar snap peas
    or mangetout
2 Little Gem lettuce, halved
    keeping the base intact
2 large slices of sourdough
80g rocket leaves
Sea salt flakes

For the dressing
4 tbsp extra virgin olive oil
4 tbsp apple cider vinegar
1 tbsp maple syrup
1 tsp wholegrain mustard
Pinch of sea salt flakes

Toppings
Fresh herbs, such as dill,
    mint, basil and or flat-
    leaf parsley, chopped
    if you like
Toasted pine nuts

A simple but absolutely delicious summery Panzanella-inspired salad with griddled Little Gem, sugar snaps and asparagus. This is a brilliant way of using up slightly stale bread, which I always seem to have. I love the way the crunchy/chewy sourdough soaks up the dressing.

You can add more leaves to make it more leaf-based, but I like to keep it quite chunky with the griddled veg and fresh herbs.

First, char the veg by adding the oil to a griddle pan on a medium heat. Add the asparagus and sugar snaps and cook for 5–6 minutes until lightly charred, turning occasionally. Scatter over some sea salt flakes and remove from the pan. Add the Little Gem and repeat.

To make the dressing, add all the ingredients to a jar. Replace the lid and shake to combine.

Toast the bread, then cut into chunky cubes.

Add the charred veg, bread and rocket to a large bowl, then pour the dressing over and toss to combine. Serve in large serving bowls, topped with the herbs, and toasted pine nuts.

Griddled Aubergine and Peanut Salad

Serves 2
Prep time 10 minutes
Cooking time 15 minutes

2 small aubergines,
   sliced lengthways
1 tbsp toasted sesame oil
1 tbsp dark soy sauce
250g cooked basmati rice
4 mini cucumbers or
   ½ cucumber, crushed
   and roughly chopped
2 spring onions, sliced
Handful of fresh coriander
Handful of salted peanuts

For the peanut dressing
2 tbsp soy sauce
1 tbsp sriracha
2 tbsp toasted sesame oil
5 tbsp coconut milk
2 tsp maple syrup
1 tsp brown rice miso paste
2 tbsp chunky peanut butter
1 tsp garlic granules
Juice of ½ lime

This dish has all my favourite flavours – smoky griddled aubergine, fresh and juicy cucumber, salted peanuts and lashings of gorgeously nutty sauce. Don't skimp on the dressing! And if you do have any left over, use it to drizzle on roast veg to make them even more delicious.

Add the sliced aubergines, toasted sesame oil and soy sauce to a bowl and toss to combine.

Heat a griddle pan on a medium heat and place a few slices of the aubergine in the pan. Turn a few times until charred and cooked through. Remove to a plate and keep warm. Repeat with the remaining slices.

To make the peanut dressing, add all the ingredients to a jar and stir to combine.

Serve the cooked rice topped with the charred aubergine slices, crushed cucumbers, spring onions, coriander, salted peanuts and lots of the dressing.

Roast Tomato and Pepper Soup with Zhoug

Serves 2–4
Prep time 10 minutes
Cooking time 35 minutes

4 tomatoes, halved
3 tbsp olive oil
1 red onion, sliced
1 tsp smoked paprika
1 tsp sweet paprika
3 garlic cloves, sliced
350g jar of roast red
    peppers, drained and
    roughly chopped
1 tbsp sun-dried tomato
    purée
125ml water
Sea salt and black pepper
Plant-based natural
    yoghurt, to serve
    (optional)

For the zhoug
1 tsp coriander seeds
1 tsp caraway seeds
½ red chilli, deseeded
    and chopped
30g fresh mint leaves
30g fresh coriander
2 large garlic cloves,
    roughly chopped
5 tbsp extra virgin olive oil,
    plus extra for topping
Juice of 1 lemon

If you think that tomato soup is boring – think again! Roasting the tomatoes to intensify their flavour and adding roast peppers and lots of smoky, warming spices elevates this soup to something special. Swirled on top is the amazing zhoug – a Yemeni herb-and-spice-packed condiment which is incredible added to soups and stews or used as a toast topper. This soup is also really lovely served chilled if you fancy a cooling summer option.

Preheat the oven to 180°C.

First, add the tomatoes and 1 tablespoon of olive oil to a medium baking tray, season with salt and pepper and roast for about 20 minutes or until soft and a little brown on the edges. Set aside.

Add the remaining 2 tablespoons of olive oil and the red onion to a medium saucepan on a medium heat and fry for 8–10 minutes until soft. Add the spices and garlic and fry for a further minute. Now, add the roast peppers, tomato purée, water, roast tomatoes and 1 teaspoon of salt and pepper and simmer for 5 minutes.

Turn off the heat and blitz with an immersion blender or in a food processor until smooth and creamy.

To make the zhoug, toast the coriander and caraway seeds in a dry frying pan on a medium heat for a couple of minutes until fragrant. Combine the toasted spices with the remaining zhoug ingredients and some seasoning in a food processor and blitz to a smooth paste. Top with a little extra olive oil.

To serve, ladle the soup into serving bowls, then top with the zhoug and some plant-based natural yoghurt, if you like.

Spiced Lentil and Tomato Soup

Serves 2
Prep time 10 minutes
Cooking time 40 minutes

2 tbsp olive oil
1 large red onion,
    roughly chopped
3 garlic cloves, sliced
2 celery sticks, diced
1 tsp ras el hanout
1 tbsp smoked paprika
4 tomatoes, roughly sliced
1 litre vegetable stock
200g dried split red
    lentils, washed
1 tbsp rose harissa
    or 1 tsp harissa paste
1 tsp sea salt
Handful of fresh mint
½ tsp chilli flakes

For the tahini dressing
2 tbsp tahini
2 tbsp olive oil
Juice of ½ lemon
2 tbsp water
Sea salt and black pepper

My favourite Moroccan-inspired soup, this dish is hearty, tasty and rich with wholesome lentils in a lovely warming spiced tomato sauce. It's really good on its own but I've added a drizzle of tahini dressing for extra creaminess.

Add the olive oil and onion to a large pan and cook on a medium heat for 7–8 minutes until soft and browning. Add the garlic and celery, stir to combine and cook for 2–3 minutes. Add the spices and stir until the vegetables are coated. Now, add the chopped tomatoes and allow them to soften a little.

Next, add the stock, lentils and harissa. Cover and simmer for 10 minutes, then remove the lid and simmer for a further 15 minutes. Season with salt and pepper.

To make the tahini dressing, add all the ingredients to a jar and mix to combine.

To serve, ladle the soup into serving bowls, drizzle with the tahini dressing and scatter over the mint, chilli flakes and sea salt.

Hearty Sweet Potato Soup

Serves 2–4
Prep time 10 minutes
Cooking time 35 minutes

1 red onion,
 roughly chopped
1 tbsp olive oil, plus
 extra for drizzling
1 tsp ground cumin
1 tsp berbere spice mix
3 garlic cloves, sliced
3 medium sweet potatoes,
 peeled and chopped
 into small cubes
1.25 litres vegetable stock
3 tbsp sun-dried
 tomato purée
Pinch of chilli flakes
 (optional)
Sea salt and black pepper

Toppings
Handful of canned
 (drained) chickpeas,
 butter beans or
 red kidney beans
Toasted seeds or dukkah
2–3 tbsp coconut
 yoghurt or coconut
 cream (optional)

This is such a lovely warming bowl of soup inspired by Ethiopian flavours. I love making a larger batch, portioning it up and freezing it for those moments when I need something fast and hearty. It's just thick enough to fill you up and the spices add layers of flavour. Serve with some fresh bread, olive oil and dukkah (see page 54).

Add the onion to a large pan with the olive oil and sauté for 10 minutes on a low heat. Add the spices and garlic and fry for a further few minutes.

Next, add the sweet potato cubes, veg stock, sun-dried tomato purée and chilli flakes (if using), cover and simmer for 20 minutes on a low heat until the sweet potato is tender. Season well.

Turn off the heat and blitz until smooth using an immersion blender.

Ladle into serving bowls and top with the chickpeas, seeds, coconut yoghurt and a drizzle of olive oil.

Quick Dinners

Three Veg Curry with Pea Mash

•

Smoky Roast Pepper and Chickpea
Stew with Dukkah

•

Gochujang Veggies with Crispy Tofu and Cashews

•

Herby Rice and Black Bean Salsa Burrito Bowl

•

Smoky Puy Lentils with Creamy Aubergine Mash

•

Dip it up Bowl – Creamy White Bean Yoghurt Dip
with Pesto and Bursting Cherry Tomatoes

Three Veg Curry with Pea Mash

Serves 2
Prep time 10 minutes
Cooking time 30 minutes

For the curry
2 tbsp olive oil
1 large red onion,
    finely diced
3 garlic cloves, sliced
1 tsp cumin seeds
1½ tsp ground turmeric
1 tsp black mustard seeds
300g cherry tomatoes,
    chopped
100ml water
1 red or orange
    pepper, deseeded
    and cubed
1 small courgette, cubed
1 small aubergine, cubed
Chilli flakes, to taste
Sea salt and black pepper

For the pea mash
450g frozen peas,
    defrosted by running
    under a hot tap in a sieve
Juice of ½ lemon
2 tbsp extra virgin olive oil

To serve
2 tbsp coconut yoghurt
    or plant-based
    natural yoghurt
Handful of chopped
    fresh coriander and mint

A simple and tasty meal absolutely packed with veg that can be whipped up in no time.

I've swapped out the traditional base of rice for a vibrant green pea mash – trust me, it works. The mash provides a creamy contrast to the warm spiced veg curry and adds plant-based protein and nutrients. A most rejuvenating meal.

To make the curry, add the oil to a large frying pan on a medium heat. Add the onion and fry for 8–10 minutes until soft and browning, then add the garlic and spices and stir for a further few minutes. Add the chopped tomatoes, water and vegetables, cover and simmer for 10–15 minutes until the vegetables are tender. Season well with chilli flakes and salt and pepper.

To make the pea mash, add all the ingredients to a food processor and blitz to a chunky mash.

To serve, top the pea mash with the veggie curry, creamy yoghurt and herbs.

Smoky Roast Pepper and Chickpea Stew with Dukkah

Serves 2
Prep time 15 minutes
Cooking time 55 minutes

6 red, orange and
   yellow mixed peppers,
   deseeded and roughly
   chopped
2 tbsp olive oil
1 red onion, roughly
   chopped
3 garlic cloves, sliced
1 tsp cumin seeds
1 tsp smoked paprika
1 tsp chipotle paste
400g can chopped
   tomatoes
400g can chickpeas,
   drained and rinsed
½ tsp sea salt flakes
   and black pepper
½ tsp chilli flakes
3 tbsp plant-based
   natural yoghurt, to serve

For the dukkah
100g hazelnuts
   or pistachios
1 tbsp cumin seeds
1 tbsp coriander seeds
3 tbsp sesame seeds
Large handful of fresh
   mint leaves
½ tsp chilli flakes
1 tsp sea salt flakes

This dish is all about the smoky roast peppers. I think it's worth roasting your own peppers, but to save time you can use pre-roasted peppers for a meal in minutes! The dukkah adds a salty, nutty crunch. Use it to top many other dishes, some of my favourites are: sprinkled on hummus on toast or over a stew or scattered on roast vegetables. The dukkah will keep up to a week stored in an airtight container.

Preheat the oven to 180°C.
   To make the dukkah, put the nuts and seeds on to a baking tray lined with baking paper. Dry toast for 10–12 minutes. Set aside to cool.
   Add the peppers to a large baking tray, drizzle over 1 tablespoon of olive oil and scatter with salt. Roast for about 30 minutes until soft and browning.
   When the peppers have about 10 minutes of cooking time left, add the remaining 1 tablespoon of oil and the onion to a wide-bottomed pan and fry the onion gently on a low heat for about 10 minutes until soft and browning. Add the garlic and spices and fry for a further 30 seconds. Add the tomatoes, roast peppers and chickpeas, cover and cook on a low heat for 10 minutes. Add 1 teaspoon of salt, some black pepper and the chilli flakes to the pan and simmer, uncovered, for a further 2 minutes.
   To finish the dukkah, add the toasted nuts and seeds and the mint leaves, chilli flakes and sea salt flakes to a mini chopper and pulse in 1-second bursts. Check after each pulse as you don't want it too finely chopped.
   Serve the stew topped with natural yoghurt and a sprinkling of dukkah.

Gochujang Veggies with Crispy Tofu and Cashews

Serves 2
Prep time 10 minutes
Cooking time 15 minutes

5 spring onions, sliced
1 tbsp coconut oil, plus
   1 tsp for the tofu
3 garlic cloves, sliced
1 tsp grated fresh ginger
1 carrot, cut into batons
½ courgette, sliced
1 red pepper, deseeded
   and sliced
380g firm tofu, drained
   well and cut into
   2cm cubes
3 tsp cashews, toasted
Handful of fresh coriander

For the sauce
3 tsp gochujang paste
3 tbsp dark soy sauce
   or tamari
3 tbsp toasted sesame oil
1 tbsp rice vinegar
1 tbsp maple syrup
Juice of 1 lime
200ml light coconut milk

So many glorious flavours and textures here: crunchy veg, crispy tofu and toasted cashews in the most delicious creamy spiced sauce. You can serve it with rice or noodles if you like, but I think it's more than substantial enough just as it is.

What's gochujang? Gochujang or red chilli paste is a savoury, sweet and spicy fermented condiment popular in Korean cooking. A brilliant ingredient for your storecupboard.

Fry the spring onions in 1 tablespoon of coconut oil in a frying pan for 4–5 minutes until soft. Add the garlic and ginger and fry for a further minute. Add the veg and stir for 4–5 minutes until just tender. Turn off the heat while you fry the tofu and make the sauce.

Heat 1 teaspoon of coconut oil in a large frying pan or wok. Fry the tofu for 1–2 minutes on each side until brown and crispy, then transfer to a plate and keep warm.

To make the sauce, add all the ingredients to a jar and mix to combine.

Add the sauce to the pan with the veg, stir to combine and turn the heat to medium. Cook for 1–2 minutes to warm through.

To serve, top the veg with the crispy tofu, toasted cashews and coriander.

Herby Rice and Black Bean Salsa Burrito Bowl

Serves 2
Prep time 10 minutes
Cooking time 5 minutes

Splash of olive oil
100g sugar snap peas
1 avocado, flesh sliced

For the rice
2 tbsp extra virgin olive oil
250g cooked basmati rice
Juice of ½ lime
1 tsp maple syrup
40g fresh herbs, such as
    coriander, flat-leaf
    parsley, mint and/or
    dill, chopped
Sea salt and black pepper

For the black bean salsa
240g canned black beans,
    drained and rinsed
2 tbsp sun-dried
    tomato paste
100g cherry tomatoes,
    chopped
Juice of ½ lime
4 tbsp fresh mint, shredded
½ tsp sea salt flakes
Pinch of chilli flakes

Both fresh and substantial, this burrito bowl is packed with fresh herbs which elevate the rice to something special. The black bean salsa just needs to be mixed and it also makes a great jacket potato topper. Feel free to serve the sugar snaps raw if you like, but charring them adds extra flavour.

To make the rice, add 1 tablespoon of the oil to a frying pan with the cooked rice, lime juice and maple syrup. Fry for 1–2 minutes on a medium heat, then add the fresh herbs. Add the remaining tablespoon of oil and season with salt and pepper. Set aside and keep warm.

Set a small frying pan or griddle pan on a medium heat. Add a splash of olive oil and the sugar snaps and fry for 2–3 minutes until a little charred.

To make the black bean salsa, add all the ingredients to a bowl and stir to combine.

To serve, load two bowls with the rice mixture, black beans salsa, sugar snaps and sliced avocado.

Smoky Puy Lentils with Creamy Aubergine Mash

Serves 2
Prep time 10 minutes plus
10 minutes cooling
Cooking time 50 minutes

1 tbsp olive oil
1 large red onion, chopped
1 large carrot, finely
    chopped
2 celery sticks, sliced
3 garlic cloves, sliced
1 tbsp smoked paprika
200g dried dark green
    French or Puy lentils,
    rinsed
3 tbsp sun-dried
    tomato purée
1.1 litres vegetable stock
1 tbsp balsamic syrup
1 tbsp vegan
    Worcestershire sauce
1 tsp light soy sauce

For the aubergine mash
2 medium aubergines
2 tbsp extra virgin olive oil
1 garlic clove, sliced
    (optional)
1 tbsp tahini
Juice of ½ lemon
1 tsp smoked paprika
1 tsp sea salt

Toppings
Fresh mint and dill,
    shredded
Plant-based natural yoghurt
Pomegranate seeds

This is the kind of stew that warms your insides and makes you happy. My Puy lentil stew is flavoured with all the umami flavours: balsamic, soy, vegan Worcestershire sauce and smoked paprika, which all add great depth. My favourite way to eat this earthy stew is on a baba ganoush-inspired aubergine mash as the contrasting textures and flavours are wonderful and add some additional veg to your meal. I also recommend adding lots of fresh herbs like shredded mint and dill. Scoop up with some fresh bread – heaven!

Preheat the oven to 180°C.

Add the oil and red onion to a wide-bottomed pan and fry gently on a low heat for about 5 minutes. Then add the carrot and celery and fry for a further 5 minutes. Add the garlic and fry for 30 seconds, then add the smoked paprika. Next, add the lentils, sun-dried tomato purée and stock and stir to combine. Bring to the boil, then cook on a low heat for 40 minutes, stirring occasionally.

Meanwhile, to make the aubergine mash, add the aubergines to a roasting tin and roast for 25–30 minutes until soft inside. Remove from the oven and leave to cool.

Once the aubergines are cool, slice through the skin and scoop out the flesh. Add the aubergine flesh and the remaining mash ingredients to a food processor or blender and blitz to a smooth paste.

Add the balsamic syrup, Worcestershire sauce and soy sauce to the lentils and stir to combine.

Serve the lentil stew on a bed of the aubergine mash and top with fresh herbs, natural yoghurt and pomegranate seeds.

Quick Dinners

Dip it up Bowl – Creamy White Bean Yoghurt Dip with Pesto and Bursting Cherry Tomatoes

Serves 2
Prep time 10 minutes
Cooking time 20 minutes

300g cherry tomatoes
1 tbsp olive oil

For the white bean yoghurt dip
240g canned butter beans, rinsed and drained
1 garlic clove
2 tbsp extra virgin olive oil
4 tbsp plant-based Greek-style yoghurt
Pinch of ground cumin
Juice of ½ lemon
Pinch each of sea salt and black pepper

For the pesto
30g fresh basil
50g pine nuts, toasted
3 tbsp extra virgin olive oil
Juice of ½ lemon
Pinch of sea salt
3 tbsp nutritional yeast
50ml water

Toppings (optional)
Fresh mint
Pinch of chilli flakes
Toasted pine nuts or sunflower seeds

You've got to love a dip. I always have at least two or three in the fridge at any time ready to be spread on toast or as a base for my meals. This one is ultra-creamy with butter beans, Greek-style yoghurt and extra virgin olive oil. Made even better with fresh pesto swirled in and topped with warm, bursting cherry tomatoes, it's heaven served with some sourdough for dunking.

Preheat the oven to 180°C.

Scatter the tomatoes over a baking tray, drizzle with the oil and season with a pinch salt. Roast for about 20 minutes or until soft and blistering.

Meanwhile, to make the white bean yoghurt dip, add all the ingredients to a food processor and blitz until very smooth and creamy. Spoon into a serving bowl.

To make the pesto, add all the ingredients to a clean food processor and blitz. Add a little more water if you prefer a looser texture.

Serve the white bean dip topped with the pesto, roast tomatoes and toppings of your choice. Mop up with fresh bread.

Restorative Bowls

Miso Noodle Broth with Smoked Tofu and Kimchi

•

Roast Root Veg Platter with Chunky Lentil Mash

•

Charred Veg Bowls with Courgette Mash and
Punchy Red Pepper Sauce

•

Edamame, Crispy Tofu and Mango Rice Bowl

•

Spinach and Tamarind Green Lentil Bowl
with Broccoli and Coconut

•

Creamy Cauliflower Rice Bowl

Miso Noodle Broth with Smoked Tofu and Kimchi

Serves 2
Prep time 10 minutes
Cooking time 25 minutes

2 tbsp olive oil
4 spring onions, sliced
3 garlic cloves, sliced
2 tsp grated fresh ginger
100g mushrooms of
    your choice, sliced
500ml vegetable stock
2 tsp brown rice miso paste
2 tsp sriracha
1 tbsp tamari
100g cherry tomatoes,
    halved
100g kimchi,
    roughly chopped
100g smoked tofu, drained
    well and cut into 1.5cm
    cubes
85g dried soba noodles or
    150g fresh rice noodles

Toppings
Shredded fresh mint and
    coriander leaves
Crushed salted peanuts

Made almost entirely from storecupboard ingredients, this is a great recipe to have for the times when you want something fast, nurturing and a little spicy! It's absolutely packed with flavour from the miso, sriracha and kimchi but is comforting with the noodles and restorative at the same time. You can add in any extra veg you like – I love to add spring greens, green beans, broccoli and asparagus.

Add the oil to a large pan on a medium heat, then add the spring onions and fry for 4–5 minutes until soft. Now, add the garlic and ginger and fry for 1 minute, then add the mushrooms. Fry for 2–3 minutes, then add all the remaining ingredients, except the noodles, and simmer, uncovered, for 15 minutes.

If using dried noodles, cook according to the pack instructions, drain and add to the pan.

For fresh noodles – add to the pan at the end and simmer for 1 minute.

Serve topped with lots of shredded herb leaves and crushed salted peanuts.

Roast Root Veg Platter with Chunky Lentil Mash

Serves 2
Prep time 15 minutes
Cooking time 50 minutes

2 carrots, scrubbed
   and sliced
2 parsnips, scrubbed
   and sliced
500g baby potatoes
1 bulb garlic, sliced in half
   through the middle
2 tbsp olive oil
Sea salt and black pepper
Fresh dill

For the lentil mash
2 leeks, washed and sliced
1 tbsp olive oil
2 tsp garam masala
1 tbsp smoked paprika
150g dried split red
   lentils, rinsed
600ml vegetable stock
2 tbsp tomato ketchup

For the tahini dressing
1 tbsp tahini
2 tbsp extra virgin olive oil
Juice of ½ lemon
Splash of water

Root vegetables are so underrated, but I love them. The magic happens when you slow roast them, so they are crispy and caramelised on the outside and soft inside. Here I've paired them with a chunky spiced lentil mash for a nourishing meal. And what can I say about the roast garlic? Squeeze it out and squish it into the lentils – so good!

Preheat the oven to 180°C.

For the roast vegetables, add the vegetables, garlic, olive oil and a pinch of salt to a large baking tray and roast for about 50 minutes or until the veg is crispy on the outside and soft on the inside.

Meanwhile, to make the lentil mash, fry the leeks in the oil in a large pan on a medium heat for 6–8 minutes until soft and browning. Add the spices and fry for a further minute. Now, add the lentils and 400ml of the stock, bring to a simmer, then gradually keep adding more stock (like a risotto) until the lentils are soft and all the stock has been absorbed. This should take about 20 minutes. Finally, stir in the tomato ketchup and season well. Take off the heat and mash with a fork – add some water if you prefer a looser texture.

To make the tahini dressing, add all the ingredients to a jar and mix to combine. Season well.

To serve, top the lentil mash with the roast root veg and garlic then drizzle over the tahini dressing and add some dill.

Restorative Bowls

Charred Veg Bowl with Courgette Mash and Punchy Red Pepper Sauce

Serves 2
Prep time 10 minutes
Cooking time 35 minutes

1 tbsp olive oil
1 orange pepper,
   deseeded and sliced into
   quarters lengthways
1 leek, washed and sliced
   in half, then down the
   middle, then cut into
   4 pieces
Handful of mangetout

For the courgette mash
2 courgettes, roughly
   chopped
1 tbsp olive oil
400g can chickpeas,
   drained and rinsed
1 garlic clove, sliced
1 tbsp tahini
Juice of ½ lemon
½ tsp sea salt and
   black pepper
Handful of fresh mint leaves
   and dill sprigs

For the red pepper sauce
2 garlic cloves
½ tsp cumin seeds
1 tsp smoked paprika
1 red pepper, chopped
½ tsp sea salt
2 tbsp white wine vinegar
4 tbsp extra virgin olive oil

This is a lovely summery dish, perfect for eating in the sun with some crispy potatoes and olive oil. It's packed with vibrant rainbow vegetables – a base of delicious courgette mash, topped with charred veggies and the punchy red pepper sauce. You can use whatever veg you like, which are great cooked on a griddle pan as here but also fantastic cooked on a BBQ.

Preheat the oven to 180°C.

To make the courgette mash, add the courgettes to a roasting tray. Toss in the oil, then roast for 25–30 minutes. Leave to cool.

Add all the courgette mash ingredients, except the herbs, but including the cooled roast courgettes to a food processor or blender and blitz to a chunky paste. Add the mint and dill and pulse briefly. Set aside.

Put a griddle pan on a medium heat, then add the olive oil, red pepper, leek and mangetout.

Cook for 3–4 minutes, turning frequently, until soft and charred.

To make the red pepper sauce, add all the ingredients to a clean food processor and blitz.

Serve the charred veg on a bed of courgette mash, topped with the red pepper sauce.

Restorative Bowls

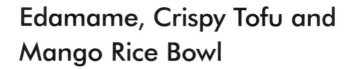

Edamame, Crispy Tofu and Mango Rice Bowl

Serves 2
Prep time 10 minutes
Cooking time 30 minutes

140g sushi rice
1 tbsp rice wine vinegar
1 tbsp olive oil
200g firm tofu, drained
  and dried well
150g frozen edamame
  beans, defrosted by
  soaking in boiling water
  for a few minutes
½ mango, peeled, stoned
  and sliced
4 tbsp kimchi
2 tsp pickled ginger
2 tbsp toasted white or
  black sesame seeds
Sea salt

For the dressing
1 tbsp rice wine vinegar
1 tbsp tamari or dark
  soy sauce
½ tsp coconut sugar
Zest and juice of ½ lime
2 tbsp toasted sesame oil
2 tbsp sriracha
1 tbsp brown rice
  miso paste
3 tbsp coconut cream
  or coconut yoghurt

This vegan dish is inspired by a Hawaiian Poke bowl but with crispy tofu in place of the fish. Lots of tasty individual elements come together here, I've included sushi rice, crispy tofu, edamame, kimchi, pickled ginger as well as a super tasty sauce packed full of umami flavours and mango for freshness. It's bold and fresh at the same time.

Cook the rice according to the pack instructions. Drain and season with salt and the rice wine vinegar.

Heat the oil in a large frying pan or wok. Slice the tofu into large cubes or triangles.

Fry the tofu for about 5–6 minutes until brown and crispy, turning frequently, then transfer to a plate.

To make the dressing, add all the ingredients to a jar and mix to combine.

In two serving bowls, present the cooked rice, crispy tofu, edamame, mango, kimchi and pickled ginger in sections, then drizzle with the dressing and scatter over the toasted sesame seeds.

Restorative Bowls

Spinach and Tamarind Green Lentil Bowl with Broccoli and Coconut

Serves 2
Prep time 10 minutes
Cooking time 45 minutes

2 tbsp olive oil
1 tbsp black mustard seeds
1 tsp cumin seeds
1 tsp ground turmeric
8 dried or fresh curry leaves
Pinch of chilli flakes
1 onion, chopped
3 garlic cloves, sliced
1 tbsp tamarind paste
150g dried green lentils, rinsed
850–950ml water
100g spinach
250ml coconut milk
1 tsp sea salt and black pepper

For the broccoli
1 tbsp olive oil
6 Tenderstem broccoli spears
3 tbsp desiccated coconut
2 tbsp salted peanuts, crushed
Juice of ½ lime
Chilli flakes, to taste
Sea salt

This dish is inspired by dal, which for me is the perfect, deliciously healthy and restorative bowl of goodness! I've used earthy green lentils here, then added in loads of spinach to create a lovely green colour and it's made rich and creamy with coconut milk. The addition of pan-fried Tenderstem broccoli, toasted desiccated coconut and crushed salted peanuts adds brilliant texture and crunch. Great served with a salad, slaw or rice.

First, add the oil to a large frying pan on a medium heat. Add the mustard seeds. When they start to pop, add the cumin seeds, turmeric, curry leaves and chilli flakes. Stir for a few seconds, then add the onion. Fry for 8–10 minutes on a low-medium heat until soft and browning.

Add the garlic and stir for a further minute or so on a low heat. Now, add the tamarind paste, lentils and 850ml of water and simmer for 25 minutes, stirring occasionally. Add the remaining water if needed.

Blitz the spinach in a food processor until roughly chopped, then add to the lentils and simmer for 5 minutes. Stir in the coconut milk, season with the salt and pepper and simmer for a further 2 minutes..

Meanwhile, for the broccoli, heat a griddle or frying pan on a medium heat, then add the oil and broccoli. Cook for 2–3 minutes on each side until charred. Set aside.

Add the desiccated coconut to a small, dry saucepan and heat gently until lightly toasted.

In a bowl, combine the broccoli, toasted coconut, peanuts, lime juice and some chilli flakes and salt. Toss to combine.

Spoon the green lentil mixture into serving bowls and top with the broccoli mixture to serve.

Restorative Bowls

Creamy Cauliflower Rice Bowl

Serves 2
Prep time 15 minutes
Cooking time 45 minutes

1 large onion,
   roughly chopped
2 tbsp olive oil
1 tsp cumin seeds
1 tsp garam masala
1 tsp smoked paprika
4 garlic cloves, sliced
400ml can light
   coconut milk
2 tbsp tomato purée
1 tsp brown rice miso paste
1 tbsp dark soy sauce
   or tamari
150g cherry tomatoes,
   halved
Sea salt
200g cooked plain or
   whole grain rice, to serve

For the roast cauliflower
1 small cauliflower,
   chopped into
   small florets
2 tbsp olive oil
Pinch of sea salt

Toppings
Fresh coriander
½ red onion, chopped

I have combined some of my favourite flavours here to create a very delicious sauce which wraps around the nutty roast cauliflower beautifully. The fresh red onion topping adds a brilliant contrast. This is exactly the kind of meal I love to eat when I need something restorative and cosy.

Preheat the oven to 180°C.

To make the roast cauliflower, add the cauliflower florets to a roasting tray, then toss in the olive oil and salt to coat. Roast for 35–40 minutes until the cauliflower is crispy on the outside.

Meanwhile, in a medium pan on a medium heat, fry the onion in the oil for 8–10 minutes until soft and browning. Add the spices and garlic, stir for a further few minutes, then add the coconut milk, tomato purée, miso, soy sauce and cherry tomatoes. Bring to a simmer and cook for 15 minutes, uncovered, then add the roast cauliflower and cook for a further 2–3 minutes. Season well with salt.

Serve with the cooked rice and top with fresh coriander and red onion.

Comfort Bowls

Spicy Black Beans with Crispy Sweet Potatoes

•

Roast Tomato and Aubergine Pesto Pasta

•

Hoisin Mushroom Noodle Bowl with Gomashio

•

Mushroom Ragù with Parsnip and Carrot Mash

•

Creamy Roast Squash Risotto with Rocket
and Hazelnuts

•

Salt and Pepper Tofu with Crispy Baby Potatoes,
Crushed Peas and Tartare Sauce

•

Coconut Veggie Curry

Spicy Black Beans with Crispy Sweet Potatoes

Serves 2
Prep time 10 minutes
Cooking time 40 minutes

2 sweet potatoes, chopped
  into 2cm cubes
1 tsp Cajun spice mix
2 tbsp olive oil
Sea salt

For the black beans
2 tbsp olive oil
1 bunch spring onions,
  chopped
4 garlic cloves, sliced
1 tsp Cajun spice mix
1 tsp cumin seeds
1 tsp ancho chilli flakes
  or chilli flakes
1 red pepper, deseeded
  and sliced into
  small pieces
250g cherry
  tomatoes, halved
400g can black beans,
  including their water
1 tsp sea salt and
  white pepper

Toppings
Plant-based natural yoghurt
Fresh mint leaves or
  oregano, chopped

This is one of my favourite easy meals to whip up from mostly storecupboard ingredients – the black beans can be swapped for red kidney beans or chickpeas so it's a very versatile dish.

The cajun spice mix infuses tons of punchy flavour into this simple bowl and I love to add crispy spiced sweet potatoes to make it into a very moreish and sustaining dish.

Preheat the oven to 180°C.

Add the sweet potatoes to a baking tray along with the Cajun spice mix, olive oil and some salt and toss to combine. Bake for 35–40 minutes or until crispy on the outside and soft in the middle.

Meanwhile, to make the black beans, add the oil to a large frying pan on a medium heat. Add the spring onions and fry for 6–8 minutes until soft and browning. Add the garlic and fry for a further minute.

Add the spices and cook for a minute or so. Add the pepper and cherry tomatoes and cook for a further 5 minutes until they have softened. Add a splash of water if needed. Now, tip in the black beans with their liquid, cover and simmer for 10 minutes. Season with the salt and pepper.

Serve the spicy black beans with the crispy sweet potatoes alongside, topped with the yoghurt and herbs.

Roast Tomato and Aubergine Pesto Pasta

Serves 2
Prep time 10 minutes
Cooking time 30 minutes

300g mixed cherry
    tomatoes
1 red pepper, deseeded
    and sliced
1 aubergine, chopped
    into 2cm cubes
1 onion, sliced
1 tbsp olive oil
250g dried conchiglioni or
    pasta of your choice
Sea salt flakes and
    black pepper
Chilli flakes, to serve

For the pesto
30g fresh basil, rocket
    or spinach
100g pine nuts, hazelnuts
    or sunflower seeds
3 tbsp extra virgin olive oil
Juice of ½ lemon
½ tsp sea salt and
    black pepper
4 tbsp nutritional yeast
50–75ml water

I love this dish, which is super simple to make but packed with flavour. A fresh and vibrant pesto with cubes of roast aubergine and peppers, comforting pasta and bursting cherry tomatoes which pop and ooze their juices into the pesto. It's incredibly tasty and utterly moreish. It's also a very flexible dish – you can use any seasonal veg you have in the fridge, it all works. And the basil in the pesto can be swapped for rocket or spinach and the pine nuts for hazelnuts or sunflower seeds.

Preheat the oven to 180°C.

Add the cherry tomatoes and vegetables to a large roasting tin, drizzle with the olive oil and season well. Roast for 25–30 minutes or until everything is soft and caramelising.

Meanwhile, cook the pasta according to the pack instructions, then drain.

To make the pesto, add all the ingredients to a food processor and blitz to combine.

To serve, fold the pesto into the cooked pasta and divide between two serving bowls. Top with the roast veg and a sprinkling of chilli flakes.

Hoisin Mushroom Noodle Bowl with Gomashio

Serves 2
Prep time 10 minutes
Cooking time 15 minutes

4 spring onions, chopped
2 tbsp coconut oil
4 garlic cloves, sliced
1 tsp grated fresh ginger
300g mushrooms of
    your choice, sliced
150g sugar snap peas
100g green beans trimmed
    and halved
300g fresh noodles of
    your choice

For the sauce
4 tbsp hoisin sauce
1 tbsp tahini
2 tbsp tamari or dark
    soy sauce
3 tbsp toasted sesame oil
1 tbsp balsamic glaze
    or good-quality
    balsamic vinegar
4 tbsp light coconut milk

For the gomashio
3 tbsp sesame seeds
½ tsp sea salt flakes

Topping
2 spring onions, sliced

Absolutely packed with umami flavours, this is a veg bowl of deliciousness. The earthy, juicy mushrooms are a great carrier for the sweet and nutty hoisin sauce and the sugar snaps and green beans add crunch along with the salty, nutty gomashio. I love to make this for friends as it's definitely a crowd-pleaser.

Fry the spring onions in the coconut oil in a large frying pan or wok on a medium heat for 5 minutes.

Add the garlic, ginger and vegetables and stir-fry for a further 3–4 minutes until the vegetables are just tender.

To make the sauce, mix the sauce ingredients in a bowl to combine, then add to the veg and simmer for 1–2 minutes.

Meanwhile, cook the noodles according to the pack instructions, then drain.

To make the gomashio, dry toast the sesame seeds on a medium heat and salt in a small pan until lightly toasted. Be careful not to let them burn. Set aside.

To serve, top the noodles with the veg, gomashio and spring onions.

Mushroom Ragù with Parsnip and Carrot Mash

Serves 2
Prep time 15 minutes
Cooking time 30 minutes

2 tbsp olive oil
1 onion, roughly sliced
1 celery stick, finely sliced
4 garlic cloves, sliced
1 tsp smoked paprika
1 tsp dried oregano
3 tbsp sun-dried
    tomato purée
250ml vegetable stock
400g mixed or wild
    mushrooms, chopped
75ml red wine
1 tbsp balsamic syrup
1 tsp dark soy sauce
3 tbsp fresh thyme
    leaves plus extra
    for topping
Sea salt and black pepper

For the mash
3 parsnips, peeled and
    cut into cubes
1 carrot, cut into cubes
2 tbsp extra virgin olive oil
3 tbsp nutritional yeast

All the lovely earthy flavours of wild mushrooms in a rich and smoky sauce which delivers delicious bold flavour. Spoon it over the vibrant, healthy parsnip and carrot mash for the perfect comfort dish to make your belly happy. The mushroom ragù is also delicious with pasta or crispy potatoes!

Add the olive oil, onion and celery to a large pan on a medium heat and fry for 8–10 minutes until very soft. Add the garlic, paprika and oregano and stir to combine, then add the sun-dried tomato purée and stock and simmer for 1–2 minutes.

Add the mushrooms and red wine, stir to combine and cook for a further 2–3 minutes. Reduce the heat and simmer for 15 minutes. Stir in the balsamic syrup, soy sauce and fresh thyme and season with salt and pepper.

Meanwhile, to make the mash, boil the parsnips and carrot in a saucepan of salted boiling water for 30 minutes or until tender.

Drain the parsnips and carrot and transfer to a food processor along with the extra virgin olive oil, nutritional yeast and some salt and pepper. Blitz until smooth and creamy, adding a little water if needed for a looser texture.

Serve the mushroom ragù on a bed of creamy mash with some thyme leaves.

Creamy Roast Squash Risotto with Rocket and Hazelnuts

Serves 2
Prep time 10 minutes
Cooking time 45 minutes

1 medium butternut
squash, peeled, deseeded
  and chopped into
  small cubes
3 tbsp olive oil
1 onion, roughly chopped
4 garlic cloves, minced
250g arborio rice
50ml white wine
1 litre hot vegetable stock
Sea salt and black pepper

For the squash purée
¾ of the roast squash (see
  above and method)
3 tbsp nutritional yeast
2 tbsp extra virgin olive oil
½ tsp sea salt
1 tsp brown rice miso paste
Juice of 1 lemon

Toppings
Handful of rocket
4 tbsp toasted hazelnuts,
  roughly chopped
Extra virgin olive oil

A vibrantly golden risotto with roast squash purée folded through, which intensifies the wonderful squash flavour, topped with peppery rocket and toasted hazelnuts for delicious crunch. And the nutritional yeast provides the all-important 'cheesy' flavour.

I also love to add some sautéed wild mushrooms or juicy roast cherry tomatoes for an extra pop of colour on top.

Preheat the oven to 180°C.

Add the butternut squash to a baking tray, then toss in 1 tablespoon of olive oil, and season with salt and pepper. Roast for about 40 minutes or until cooked and golden brown. Remove from the oven and reserve one quarter of the roast squash; keep warm

Meanwhile, to make the risotto, add the remaining 2 tablespoons of oil to a frying pan on a low-medium heat, then add the onion and fry for 8–10 minutes until soft. Next, add the garlic and fry for a minute or so. Now, add the rice and stir to combine thoroughly. Add the white wine and cook until it has completely evaporated. Slowly add a ladleful of stock at a time, until absorbed, then add the next ladleful.

In the meantime, make the squash purée by adding the remaining three-quarters of the roast squash and the rest of the purée ingredients to a food processor and blitzing until smooth and creamy.

Continue to add the stock to the risotto until it's all been absorbed and the risotto looks thick and creamy. Add the squash purée, stir to combine and cook for 1–2 minutes to heat through. Season with salt and pepper and turn off the heat.

To serve, divide the risotto between two serving bowls, top with the reserved roast squash, the rocket, toasted hazelnuts, a drizzle of extra virgin olive oil and some sea salt.

Salt and Pepper Tofu with Crispy Baby Potatoes, Crushed Peas and Tartare Sauce

Serves 2
Prep time 15 minutes
Cooking time 50 minutes

350g baby potatoes
2 tbsp olive oil
2 tbsp sunflower
or vegetable oil
396g pack firm tofu,
drained and dried well
2 tbsp cornflour
½ tsp Chinese 5 spice
½ tsp seaweed flakes
(optional)
Sea salt and black pepper

For the tartare sauce
3 tbsp plant-based natural
yoghurt
Juice of ¼ lemon
1 tsp maple syrup
7 cocktail gherkins, finely
chopped
3 tsp mini capers
2 tbsp chopped fresh dill

For the crushed peas
200g frozen peas,
defrosted
3 tbsp extra virgin olive oil
Squeeze of lemon juice

This is kind of a vegan fish and chips with the crispy salt and pepper tofu instead of the fish alongside crispy potatoes, crushed peas and a zingy tartare sauce. The seaweed flakes used to coat the tofu are optional but add a 'fishy' flavour and work really well with the Chinese 5 spice. This delicious meal has plenty of plant-based protein from the tofu and peas to keep you feeling fuller for longer.

Preheat the oven to 180°C.

Add the potatoes, olive oil and a big pinch of salt to a large baking tray and roast for about 50 minutes or until crispy on the outside and soft on the inside. Turn occasionally.

Meanwhile, preheat a griddle pan on a medium heat and add the sunflower oil. Cut the tofu in half down the centre like a book. Cut each piece into four triangles, to give you 8 pieces in total. Mix together the cornflour, 5 spice, seaweed flakes (if using), ½ teaspoon of salt and ½ teaspoon of pepper on a plate. Gently turn each piece of tofu in the cornflour mixture to coat. Add the tofu pieces to the griddle pan (in two batches, if necessary) and cook until nicely charred on each side.

To make the tartare sauce, add all the ingredients to a bowl, season and mix to combine.

For the crushed peas, add all the ingredients to a bowl, season and mix to combine, then crush the peas roughly with a fork.

Serve the potatoes, tofu, crushed peas and tartare sauce together in two serving bowls.

Coconut Veggie Curry

Serves 2
Prep time 10 minutes
Cooking time 25 minutes

400ml can light
    coconut milk
100ml water
1 tsp tamarind paste
1 sweet potato, peeled and
    cut into 2cm cubes
130g Tenderstem broccoli
75g baby corn, sliced
    lengthways
Crushed salted peanuts,
    and chilli flakes
    to serve

For the curry paste
3 tbsp desiccated coconut
3 garlic cloves, peeled
1 echalion shallot, chopped
1 lemongrass stalk,
    tough outer layer
    removed, sliced
1 red chilli, deseeded
1 thumb-sized piece of
    fresh ginger, peeled and
    roughly chopped
1 tsp ground turmeric
½ tsp ground cinnamon
1 tsp sea salt
2 tsp light soft brown sugar
2 tbsp vegetable oil

A coconut veggie curry to make you smile. All you need to do is whip up the fragrant paste, add to your pan with some coconut milk and then simmer the veg until tender. Top with some crushed salted peanuts to add essential crunch and enjoy!

First, make the curry paste. Add the coconut to a dry pan and cook until it's lightly toasted. Add to a food processor along with all the remaining paste ingredients and blitz to a chunky paste.

Heat a frying pan on a medium heat, then add the curry paste and fry for 2–3 minutes. Now, add the coconut milk, water, tamarind paste and sweet potato. Cover and simmer for 10 minutes, then add the broccoli and baby corn. Cover and simmer for a further 5 minutes or until the veg is just tender.

Serve topped with the crushed peanuts and chilli flakes for an extra pop of colour, if you fancy.

Dessert Bowls

Chocolate Mousse Pots with Raspberry Sauce

•

Caramel Pear, Pecan Crumble and Lemon
Yoghurt Parfait Bowls

•

Plum, Blackberry and Tahini Crumble

•

Coconut Sticky Rice Pudding with Mango

•

Orange Posset with Warm Cherries

•

Apple and Date Pot Pies

Chocolate Mousse Pots with Raspberry Sauce

Makes 4 mini or 2 large
chocolate pots
Prep time 10 minutes plus
2-3 hours chilling
Cooking time 5 minutes

160ml aquafaba –
   liquid from 400g
   can chickpeas
1 tsp apple cider vinegar
200g dairy-free
   dark chocolate
2 tbsp coconut oil
1 tbsp raw cacao
7 tbsp maple syrup
1 tsp vanilla extract
Pinch of sea salt flakes

For the raspberry sauce
300g raspberries
Splash of maple syrup

This is an easy but a rather grown-up little dessert. Rich and dense chocolate decadence topped with slightly tart raspberries – it's very good. If you haven't tried aquafaba before, maybe this will convince you. Don't worry if you can't get fluffy peaks when you whip it up – the mousse will still be wonderful.

Whip the aquafaba with the vinegar in a large bowl, using a whisk or an immersion blender. Whisk for 2–3 minutes until fluffy – don't worry if it doesn't thicken into peaks.

Break up the chocolate and add to a saucepan with the coconut oil. Heat very gently on a low heat until melted. Don't over-stir. Turn off the heat, allow to cool a little, then gently stir in the remaining ingredients (except the whipped aquafaba) to combine well.

Spoon the chocolate mix into the whipped aquafaba. Gently mix together to combine. Carefully spoon into glasses and place in the fridge for 2–3 hours to firm up.

Meanwhile, to make the raspberry sauce, add the berries and maple syrup to a saucepan and simmer until they have broken down a little. Sieve to remove the seeds, if you prefer. Leave to cool.

To serve, top the chocolate pots with the raspberry sauce.

Dessert Bowls

Caramel Pear, Pecan Crumble and Lemon Yoghurt Parfait Bowls

Serves 2–4
Prep time 10 minutes
Cooking time 10 minutes

4 ripe pears, peeled, cored
and cut into 1cm cubes
2 tbsp dark soft
brown sugar
100ml water

For the pecan crumble
6 tbsp ground almonds
2 tbsp plain flour
3 tbsp pecans
2 tbsp chopped nuts,
such as almonds and/
or hazelnuts
3 tbsp maple syrup

For the lemon yoghurt
6 tbsp plant-based Greek-
style or natural yoghurt
2 tbsp maple syrup
Zest and juice of 1 lemon
Pinch of ground turmeric

Layers of sweet and soft pears with fresh, zingy lemon yoghurt and a gorgeously nutty crunchy crumble layer. That's why I love parfaits – every mouthful is a little different with smooth, creamy and crispy textures. This is the kind of dessert which can also be eaten for breakfast if you have any leftovers – lovely with a splash of oat milk. Pears are delicious but apples work just as well here, and I also love to add some berries and jammy dates or figs.

Preheat the oven to 180°C.

In a bowl, mix together all the pecan crumble ingredients until combined, then transfer to a medium baking tray. Bake for 10 minutes until lightly toasted. Set aside.

Meanwhile, add the pears, sugar and water to a small saucepan, cover and simmer on a medium heat for 10 minutes until tender. Set aside.

To make the lemon yoghurt layer, mix all the ingredients together in a small bowl.

To serve, layer half the pears and pecan crumble into two medium or four small pots or glasses. Add half the lemon yoghurt, then repeat so that you have six layers.

Plum, Blackberry and Tahini Crumble

Serves 2–4
Prep time 10 minutes
Cooking time 25 minutes

For the crumble
100g ground almonds
6 tbsp oats of your choice
3 tbsp sunflower seeds
1 tsp ground allspice
1 tsp ground cardamom
½ tsp sea salt
2 tbsp tahini
2 tbsp peanut or
    almond butter
3 tbsp maple syrup
1 tsp vanilla extract

For the fruit layer
6 plums, stoned and sliced
150g blackberries
½ tsp ground cinnamon
4 tbsp maple syrup
Splash of water

Plant-based natural
    yoghurt,custard or
    ice cream, to serve

This classic crumble has a few twists which make it extra special. The gooey, oozy fruit base is made from plums and blackberries, then topped with a lovely nutty tahini and peanut butter topping – no flour needed. Absolutely perfect for when you want something super cosy and delicious. I love to serve it warm with cold and creamy plant-based yoghurt, custard or ice cream.

Preheat the oven to 180°C.

To make the crumble, mix the dry ingredients together in a bowl. In a small bowl, mix together the tahini, peanut butter, maple syrup and vanilla. Add the wet mixture to the dry mixture and stir thoroughly until it resembles crumbs – get your hands involved. Set aside.

To make the fruit layer, in a saucepan, combine the plums, blackberries, cinnamon, maple syrup and water. Cook on a medium heat, stirring occasionally, for 5–6 minutes until the fruit softens and there's lots of juice (reserve some to pour over the top to serve).

Now, add the fruit to two small ovenproof bowls, then add the crumble topping. Bake for 15–18 minutes until the topping is golden.

Remove from the oven and allow to cool a little. Serve with plant-based natural yoghurt, custard or ice cream and some of the reserved fruit juice.

Coconut Sticky Rice Pudding with Mango

Serves 4
Prep time 10 minutes, plus cooling
Cooking time 45 minutes

100g pudding rice
1 litre plant-based coconut milk drink
5 tbsp light soft brown sugar
1 tsp vanilla extract
3 tbsp desiccated coconut, toasted
4 tbsp coconut milk or cream

Toppings
1 mango, peeled, stoned and sliced
1 tbsp sesame seeds
1 tbsp pistachios, roughly chopped
Coconut cream

Inspired by Thai sticky coconut rice, this dessert bowl features delicious balls of sweet coconut rice flavoured with coconut milk, which makes them gorgeously creamy. Adding the toasted desiccated coconut gives extra nutty coconut flavour – just lovely. Top with some fresh mango, sesame seeds, pistachios and a spoon of coconut cream for a deliciously tropical feel.

If you don't eat all the rice immediately, store in the fridge to eat cold for breakfast – heaven!

In a medium pan, combine the rice, plant-based milk drink and sugar and stir well. Bring to the boil, then reduce the heat and cook gently for 40 minutes, stirring occasionally, until the rice is tender and has thickened. Stir in the vanilla extract, toasted desiccated coconut and coconut milk or cream. Leave to cool.

Scoop out the sticky rice and serve in small bowls topped with the mango, sesame seeds, roughly chopped pistachios and a spoonful of coconut cream.

Dessert Bowls

Orange Posset with Warm Cherries

Serves 4
Prep time 10 minutes plus 2 hours chilling
Cooking time 5 minutes

350g silken tofu
3 tbsp coconut oil, melted
2 tbsp plant-based
   Greek-style yoghurt
1 tsp vanilla extract
1 tsp orange extract
Zest and juice of ½ orange
Juice of ½ lemon
5 tbsp maple syrup

Toppings
200g cherries, stoned
   and halved
1 tbsp maple syrup
Pecan crumble (see
   page 104)

A fresh and summery dessert – creamy orange-flavoured posset topped with contrasting warm cherries and a sprinkle of nutty crumble for some crunch. The secret ingredient – silken tofu – makes it beautifully smooth and creamy. This dessert is perfect for entertaining as it's super easy to make and looks really pretty served in cute dessert bowls.

To make the posset, add the silken tofu and all the remaining ingredients to a food processor and mix until smooth and creamy. Divide between four small dessert bowls and transfer to the fridge for about 2 hours to firm up.

To make the warm cherries, add the cherries and maple syrup to a small saucepan and cook on a medium heat for 2–3 minutes until broken down a little.

To serve, top the possets with the warm cherries and a little pecan crumble.

Dessert Bowls

Apple and Date Pot Pies

Makes 3–4 pot pies
Prep time 15 minutes
Cooking time 20 minutes

1 sheet vegan puff pastry
Sunflower oil, for greasing
Sprinkle of caster sugar
Vegan ice cream or plant-
    based Greek-style
    yoghurt, to serve

For the filling
2 tbsp unsalted
    vegan butter
4 apples, peeled, cored
    and cut into 2cm cubes
4 tbsp light soft
    brown sugar
2 tbsp plain flour, plus
    extra for dusting
½ tsp ground cinnamon
200ml water
4 Medjool dates, pitted
    and finely chopped
½ tsp ground cloves
1 tsp vanilla extract

Warming, comforting apple and sticky date pot pies. Delicious, and they can be whipped up in 35 minutes! The bottom layer of gooey, warm, spiced apples is topped with a little cheat – shop-bought vegan puff pastry which puffs up in the oven in just 12–14 minutes. Pure comfort!

Preheat the oven to 220°C.

Add all the filling ingredients to a saucepan and stir to combine. Cover and simmer on a medium heat for 7–8 minutes or until the apples are tender, stirring occasionally.

Roll out the puff pastry on a lightly floured surface and cut out 3–4 circles the same size as your individual pot tops.

Divide the filling between the ovenproof pots. Place the pastry lids on top and pinch in the sides to close. Rub a little oil on top and sprinkle with caster sugar. Pierce the lids a couple of times and bake for 12–14 minutes until the pastry has puffed up and is golden on top.

Delicious served with vegan ice cream or plant-based Greek-style yoghurt.

Eat a Rainbow

Coloured foods contain important nutrients that the body needs. Here are some of the colours in this book – try and eat as many colours as you can throughout your day.

RED
Tomatoes, red lentils, red onions, red peppers, pomegranate seeds, raspberries, apples.

ORANGE
Nectarines, peaches, carrots, butternut squash, orange peppers, sweet potatoes, oranges.

YELLOW
Bananas, potatoes, yellow peppers,
parsnips, cauliflower, mango, pears,
lemons, baby corn, chickpeas.

GREEN
Matcha, pistachios, coriander, chives, parsley, dill,
mint, courgettes, asparagus, spring greens, avocado,
peas, broccoli, sugar snaps, kale, spinach, cucumber,
lettuce, mangetout, celery, green lentils, edamame
beans, gherkins, capers basil, leeks, spring onions.

INDIGO
Blackberries, cherries,
plums, aubergines.

Rainbow Planner

Use this planner to help you keep track of your rainbow foods
– try and aim for at least five different colours a day.

	MONDAY	TUESDAY	WEDNESDAY

THURSDAY	FRIDAY	SATURDAY	SUNDAY

Rainbow Planner

Use this planner to help you keep track of your rainbow foods
– try and aim for at least five different colours a day.

	MONDAY	TUESDAY	WEDNESDAY

THURSDAY	FRIDAY	SATURDAY	SUNDAY

Use this space to jot down your favourites!

Index

Index

Index

Thank yous

A few thank yous. Firstly, to my wonderful recipe testers and feedback givers aka mainly my sister Ems, Craig, my friends and mum.

I created this book half in my sister's kitchen and half in the lovely new one which my amazing step dad Maurice made for me. During the kitchen building and book development process, I lured him in with the enticing smells and he tried my mushroom ragù – the sceptic was converted!

Also thank you to Malin for her big brain, inspiration and insight. And Amanda for her on-going support, creatively and being on my team despite any challenge.

Finally thank you to all my wonderful followers and fellow veg lovers – I created this book for you.

Pop Press, an imprint of Ebury Publishing,
20 Vauxhall Bridge Road,
London SW1V 2SA

Pop Press is part of the Penguin Random House group of companies
whose addresses can be found at global.penguinrandomhouse.com

Penguin
Random House
UK

First published by Ebury Press in 2022

www.penguin.co.uk

A CIP catalogue record for this book is available from the British Library

ISBN 9781529148657

Colour origination by BORN Ltd

Printed and bound in Latvia by Livonia Print SIA

The authorised representative in the EEA is Penguin Random House Ireland,
Morrison Chambers, 32 Nassau Street, Dublin D02 YH68

MIX
Paper from
responsible sources
FSC® C018179

Penguin Random House is committed to a sustainable future for our
business, our readers and our planet. This book is made from Forest
Stewardship Council® certified paper.